yukismart.com/b/6dba06
AF364382
1
2

cat
แมว
maeo

dog
สุนัข
sunak

fish

ปลา

pla

bird

นก

nok

hen
แม่ไก่
mae kai

rooster
ไก่ตัวผู้
kaituaphu

chick
ลูกไก่
lukkai

egg
ไข่
khai

cow
วัว

wua

sheep
แกะ

kae

pig
หมู

mu

goat
แพะ

phae

horse

ม้า

ma

donkey

ลา

la

mouse

หนู

nu

rabbit

กระต่าย

kratai

turkey
ไก่งวง
kainguang

goose
ห่าน
han

peacock
นกยูง
nokyung

duck

เป็ด

pet

duckling

ลูกเป็ด

luk pet

swan

หงส์

hong

dragonfly

แมลงปอ

malaengpo

fly

แมลงวัน

malaengwan

ant

มด

mot

anteater

ตัวกินมด

tuakinmot

ladybug
แมลงเต่าทอง
malaengtaothong

earthworm
ไส้เดือน
saiduean

slug
ทาก
thak

caterpillar

หนอนผีเสื้อ

nonphisuea

snail

หอยทาก

hoithak

butterfly

ผีเสื้อ

phisuea

grasshopper

ตั๊กแตน

takkataen

bee

ผึ้ง

phueng

honey

น้ำผึ้ง

namphueng

spider

แมงมุม

maengmum

grass

หญ้า

ya

beetle

ด้วง

duang

mosquito

ยุง

yung

scorpion

แมงป่อง

maengpong

lizard

กิ้งก่า

kingka

turtle

เต่า

tao

crab

ปู

pu

shrimp

กุ้ง

kung

lobster

กุ้งมังกร

kungmangkon

whale

วาฬ

wan

shark

ปลาฉลาม

plachalam

stingray

ปลากระเบน

plakraben

dolphin

โลมา

loma

sea urchin
เม่นทะเล
menthale

jellyfish
แมงกะพรุน
maengkaphrun

squid
ปลาหมึก
plamuek

starfish

ปลาดาว

pladao

seagull

นกนางนวล

noknangnuan

sea

ทะเล

thale

pelican

นกกระทุง

nokkrathung

cormorant

นกอ้ายงั่ว

nok-aingua

shells

เปลือกหอย

plueakhoi

sand

ทราย

sai

elephant

ช้าง

chang

zebra

ม้าลาย

malai

giraffe

ยีราฟ

yirap

snake

งู

ngu

crocodile

จระเข้

chorakhe

lion

สิงโต

singto

tiger

เสือ

suea

hippopotamus
ฮิปโปโปเตมัส
hippopotemat

rhinoceros
แรด
raet

cheetah

เสือชีตาห์

sueachita

camel

อูฐ

ut

antelope

ละมั่ง

lamang

flamingo

นกฟลามิงโก้

nok fla ming ko

ostrich

นกกระจอกเทศ

nokkrachokthet

stork

นกกระสา

nokkrasa

parrot
นกแก้ว
nokkaeo

gorilla
กอริลลา
korinla

monkey
ลิง
ling

koala
โคอาล่า
kho-a la

panda
หมีแพนด้า
miphaenda

kangaroo
จิงโจ้
chingcho

hedgehog

เม่น

men

squirrel

กระรอก

krarok

wolf

หมาป่า

mapa

fox

สุนัขจิ้งจอก

sunakchingchok

racoon

แรคคูน

rae

bear

หมี

mi

deer

กวาง

kwang

eagle

นกอินทรี

nok-insi

bat
ค้างคาว
khangkhao

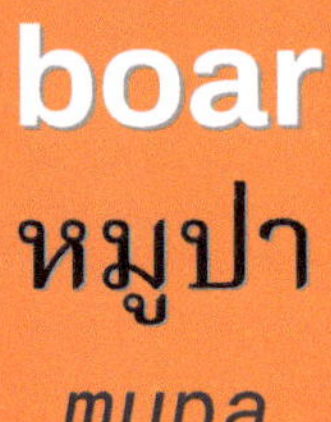

boar
หมูปา
mupa

crow
อีกา
ika

owl
นกฮูก
nokhuk

woodpecker
นกหัวขวาน
nokhuakhwan

polecat
พังพอนเหม็น
phangphon men

mole
ตุ่น
tun

beaver
บีเวอร์
bi woe

polar bear
หมีขั้วโลก
mikhualok

snow
หิมะ
hima

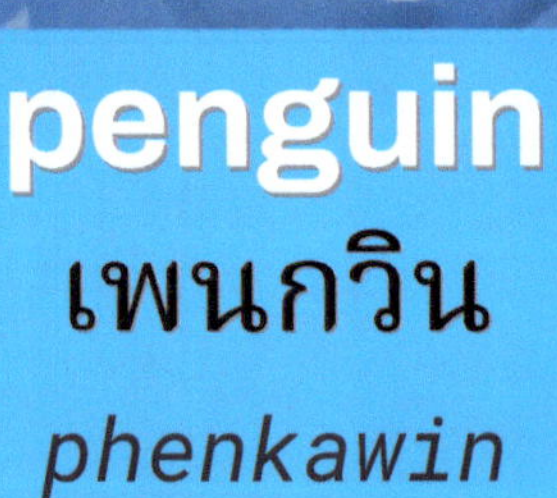

penguin
เพนกวิน
phenkawin

snowy owl
นกเค้าแมวหิมะ
nokkhaomaeo hima

forest

ปา

pa

mountain

ภูเขา

phukhao

narwhal
วาฬนาร์วาล
wan na wan

orca
วาฬเพชฌฆาต
wanphetchakhat

walrus
วอลรัส
wonrat

seal
แมวน้ำ
maeonam

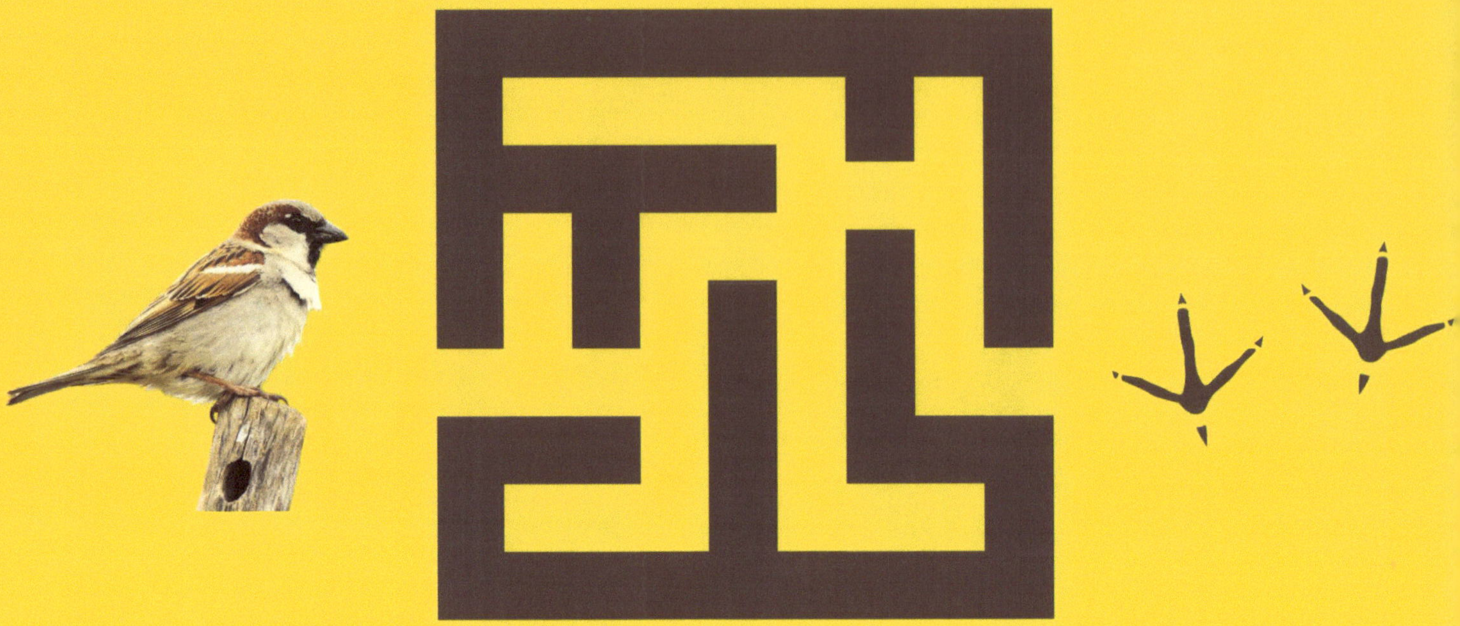